AWESOME DOGS

Maltese

by Kaitlyn Duling

BELLWETHER MEDIA · MINNEAPOLIS, MN

Note to Librarians, Teachers, and Parents:

Blastoff! Readers are carefully developed by literacy experts and combine standards-based content with developmentally appropriate text.

Level 1 provides the most support through repetition of high-frequency words, light text, predictable sentence patterns, and strong visual support.

Level 2 offers early readers a bit more challenge through varied simple sentences, increased text load, and less repetition of high-frequency words.

Level 3 advances early-fluent readers toward fluency through increased text and concept load, less reliance on visuals, longer sentences, and more literary language.

Level 4 builds reading stamina by providing more text per page, increased use of punctuation, greater variation in sentence patterns, and increasingly challenging vocabulary.

Level 5 encourages children to move from "learning to read" to "reading to learn" by providing even more text, varied writing styles, and less familiar topics.

Whichever book is right for your reader, Blastoff! Readers are the perfect books to build confidence and encourage a love of reading that will last a lifetime!

This edition first published in 2020 by Bellwether Media, Inc.

No part of this publication may be reproduced in whole or in part without written permission of the publisher. For information regarding permission, write to Bellwether Media, Inc., Attention: Permissions Department, 6012 Blue Circle Drive, Minnetonka, MN 55343.

Library of Congress Cataloging-in-Publication Data

Names: Duling, Kaitlyn, author.
Title: Maltese / by Kaitlyn Duling.
Description: Minneapolis, MN : Bellwether Media, Inc., [2020] |
   Series: Blastoff! readers: awesome dogs | Includes bibliographical references and index. | Audience: Ages 5-8 |
   Audience: Grades K-1 | Summary: "Relevant images match informative text in this introduction to Maltese dogs.
   Intended for students in kindergarten through third grade"– Provided by publisher.
Identifiers: LCCN 2019024911 (print) | LCCN 2019024912 (ebook) |
   ISBN 9781644871157 (library binding) | ISBN 9781618917652 (ebook)
Subjects: LCSH: Maltese dog–Juvenile literature.
Classification: LCC SF429.M25 D85 2020 (print) | LCC SF429.M25 (ebook) | DDC 636.76–dc23
LC record available at https://lccn.loc.gov/2019024911
LC ebook record available at https://lccn.loc.gov/2019024912

Editor: Rebecca Sabelko   Designer: Laura Sowers

Printed in the United States of America, North Mankato, MN.

Table of Contents

What Are Maltese?

Maltese are a small, friendly dog **breed**. They love to play.

These bold dogs love to run. This helps them on **agility** courses!

agility course

Maltese have round heads
and small ears. Their little noses
and gentle eyes are black.

Maltese Profile

dark eyes

white, silky coat

plumed tail

short legs

Life Span: 12 to 15 years

Trainability:

1	2	3	4	5	6

Hardest to train   Easiest to train

They have short, **sturdy** legs.
Many have **plumed** tails.

Maltese are small dogs.

They grow up to 9 inches
(23 centimeters) tall.
They weigh less than 7 pounds
(3 kilograms).

Long, Silky Coats

topknots

Maltese have straight, white **coats**. Their silky hair can be short or long.

Maltese Hairstyles

short hair   long hair

Long-haired Maltese can wear **topknots**. These dogs must be brushed often.

History of Maltese

Maltese get their name from the island of Malta.

Malta

Thousands of years ago, Malta was famous for its silks and spices. Maltese dogs were also famous!

Maltese were popular in Greece, Rome, and Egypt. Egyptians thought Maltese could cure sickness. Romans wrote poems about them.

Mary, Queen of Scots

Later, British **royals** kept them as pets.

Maltese came to the United States in the 1870s. Many people called them Maltese Lion Dogs.

They joined the **Toy Group** of the **American Kennel Club** in 1888.

Maltese are good watchdogs. They are fearless and **alert**.

They also make comforting **therapy dogs**. They love to sit on laps and cuddle.

Maltese may be small,
but they are lively
and full of fun.

Making friends is what
these dogs do best!

Glossary

agility—a dog sport in which dogs run through a series of obstacles

alert—quick to notice or act

American Kennel Club—an organization that keeps track of dog breeds in the United States

breed—a type of dog

coats—the hair or fur covering some animals

plumed—related to a section of long, fluffy fur

royals—kings, queens, and other members of ruling families

sturdy—strongly built

therapy dogs—dogs that comfort people who are sick, hurt, or have a disability

topknots—knots of hair at the top of the head tied with a bow or ribbon

Toy Group—a group of the smallest dog breeds; most dogs in the Toy Group were bred to be companions.

To Learn More

AT THE LIBRARY
Gagne, Tammy. *The Dog Encyclopedia for Kids.* North Mankato, Minn.: Capstone Young Readers, 2017.

Mills, Andrea. *The Everything Book of Dogs and Puppies.* New York, N.Y.: DK, 2018.

Schuetz, Kari. *Shih Tzus.* Minneapolis, Minn.: Bellwether Media, 2017.

ON THE WEB

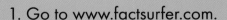

FACTSURFER

Factsurfer.com gives you a safe, fun way to find more information.

1. Go to www.factsurfer.com.

2. Enter "Maltese" into the search box and click 🔍.

3. Select your book cover to see a list of related web sites.

Index